Tom is in a tub. Tom has fun in the tub.

A frog is in the tub.
A frog is on Tom.

Help, help, help,
frogs, help.

The big pig runs to the tub to help Tom.

Bump. Bang. The big pig hits the tub.

Oh no! Oh no!
The tub tips up.

Tom and the frogs tip out of the tub.

The frogs hop and jump on the big pig.